THE

AFR🪐FUTURIST

COLORING BOOK

FORD KELLY

Bibliografische Information der Deutschen Nationalbibliothek: Die Deutsche Nationalbibliothek verzeichnet diese Publikation in der Deutschen Nationalbibliografie; detaillierte bibliografische Daten sind im Internet über dnb.dnb.de abrufbar.

Text, Layout and Illustrations: Ford Kelly

Herstellung und Verlag: BoD – Books on Demand, Norderstedt

ISBN: 978-3-7526-9110-8 (The Afrofuturist Coloring Book)

Disclaimer: Dies ist ein Werk der Afrofiction. Figuren, Orte und Szenarien sind entweder Produkte der Fantasie des Künstler:in oder fiktiv. Jegliche Ähnlichkeit mit lebenden oder von uns gegangenen Personen, Ereignissen oder Szenarien entspringt dem Zufall. Sollte eines dieser Bilder in irgendeiner Weise der Zukunft entsprechen, wäre auch dies ein großer Zufall.

THE AFROFUTURIST

COLORING BOOK

FORD KELLY

Afrofuturism plays with the past, present and the future, where time is adapted and augmented to reconsider how our realities and identities are constructed. It can be used to relate to images of mysticism, spirituality and the superhuman and acts as a form of escapism. It embodies the alien, the cyborg, the witch, the serpent and beyond. Where technology meets culture and social and political climates are redefined.

Afrofuturism gives those in the African diaspora the possibility to stretch their imagination and reimagine a future where Black people have not only survived but have thrived. One where Black queer and trans people also have central roles. One where Myths and legends are merged into new realms. Where Representation can be explored and reexamined.

This Coloring book takes you on an adventure to realms where Africa and the diaspora intertwine. Take a moment in your day to escape into the book's 27 illustrated drawings, pick your medium of choice whether crayons or coloring pens and let the pages inspire you.

Coloring books are for all ages to enjoy!

Have fun!

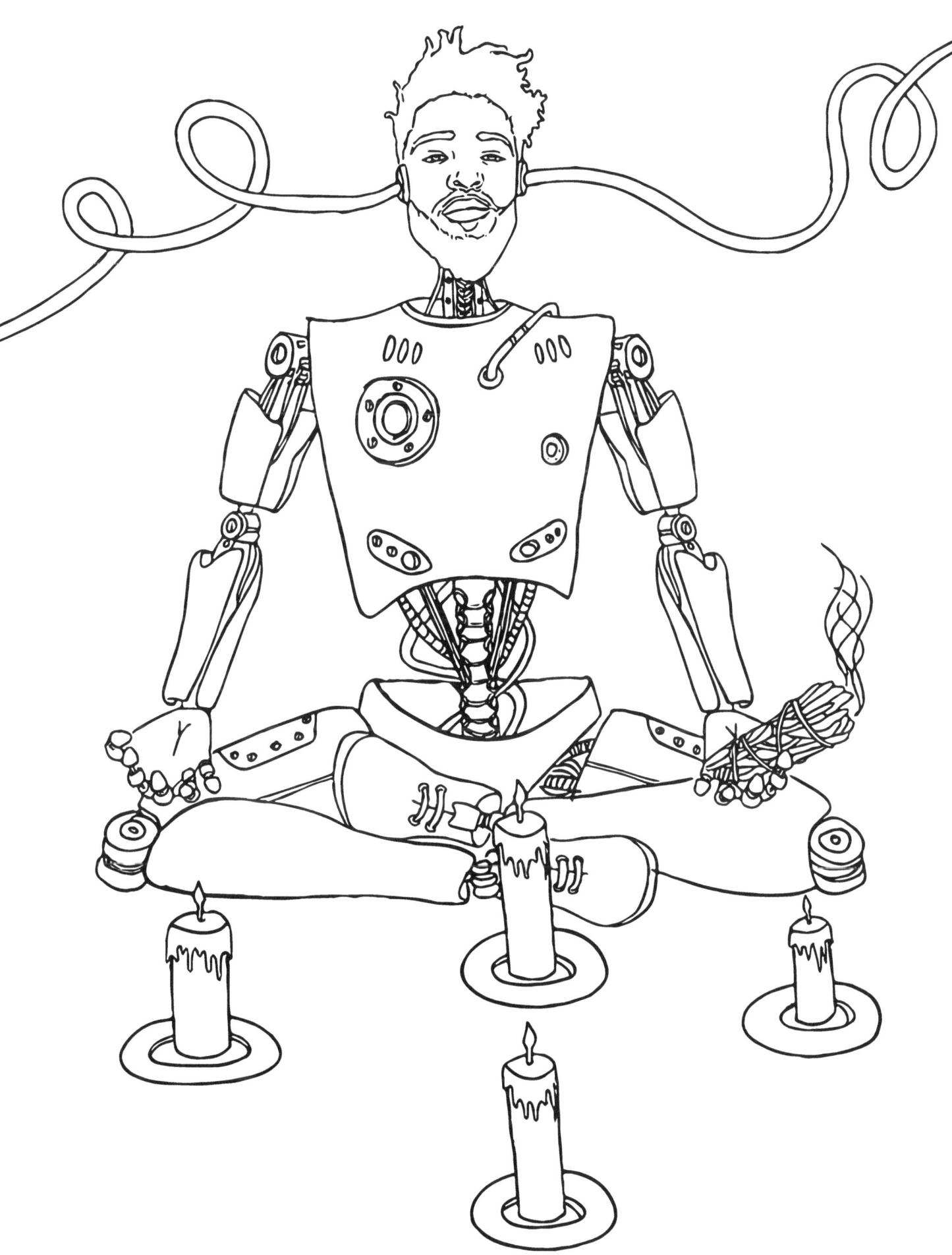

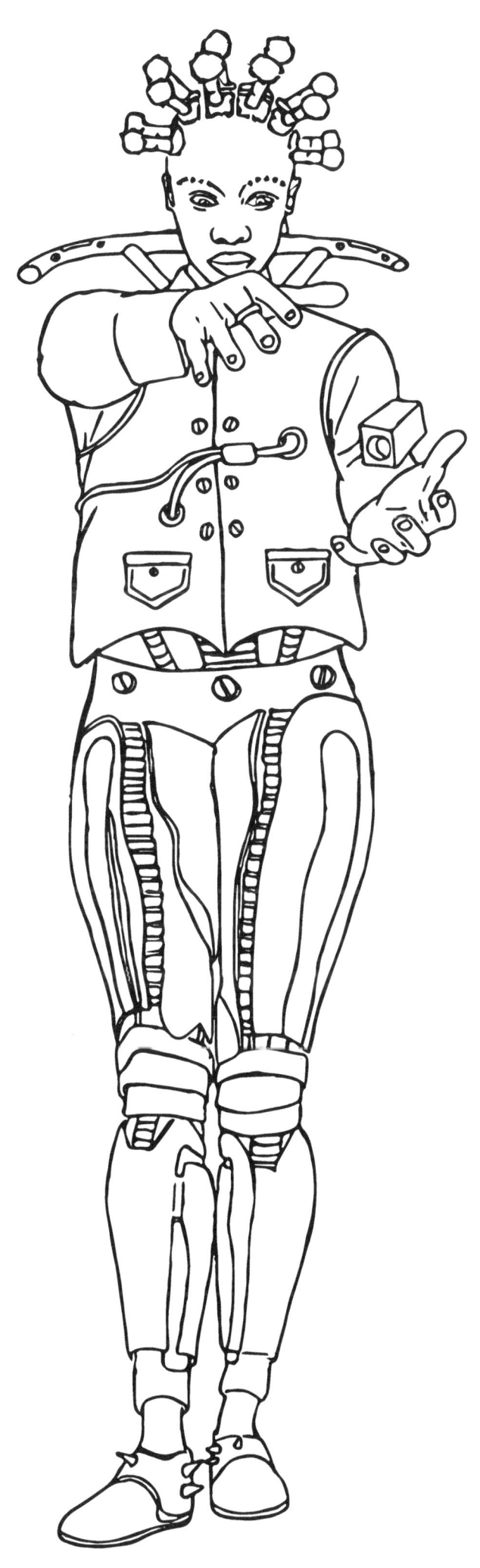

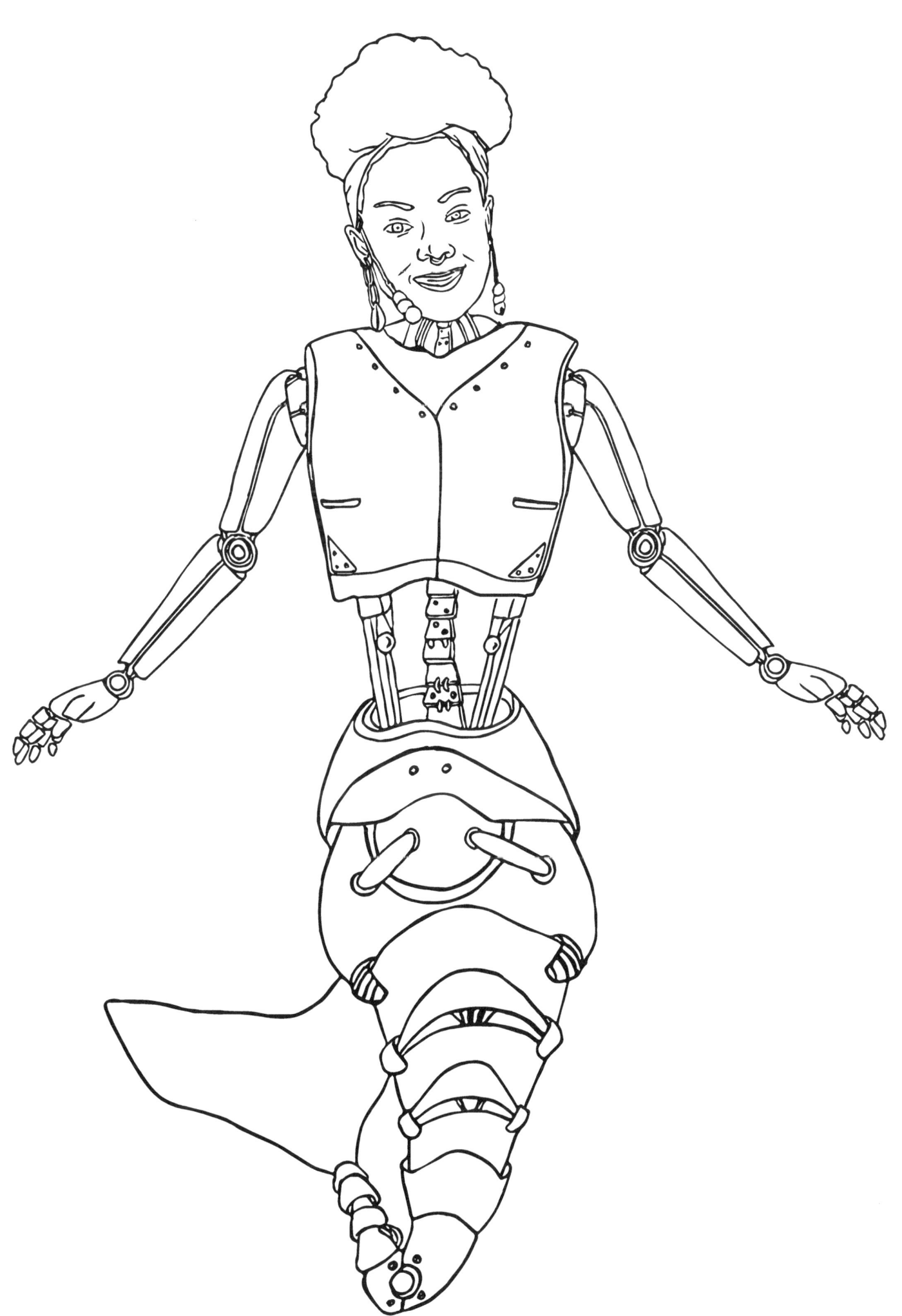

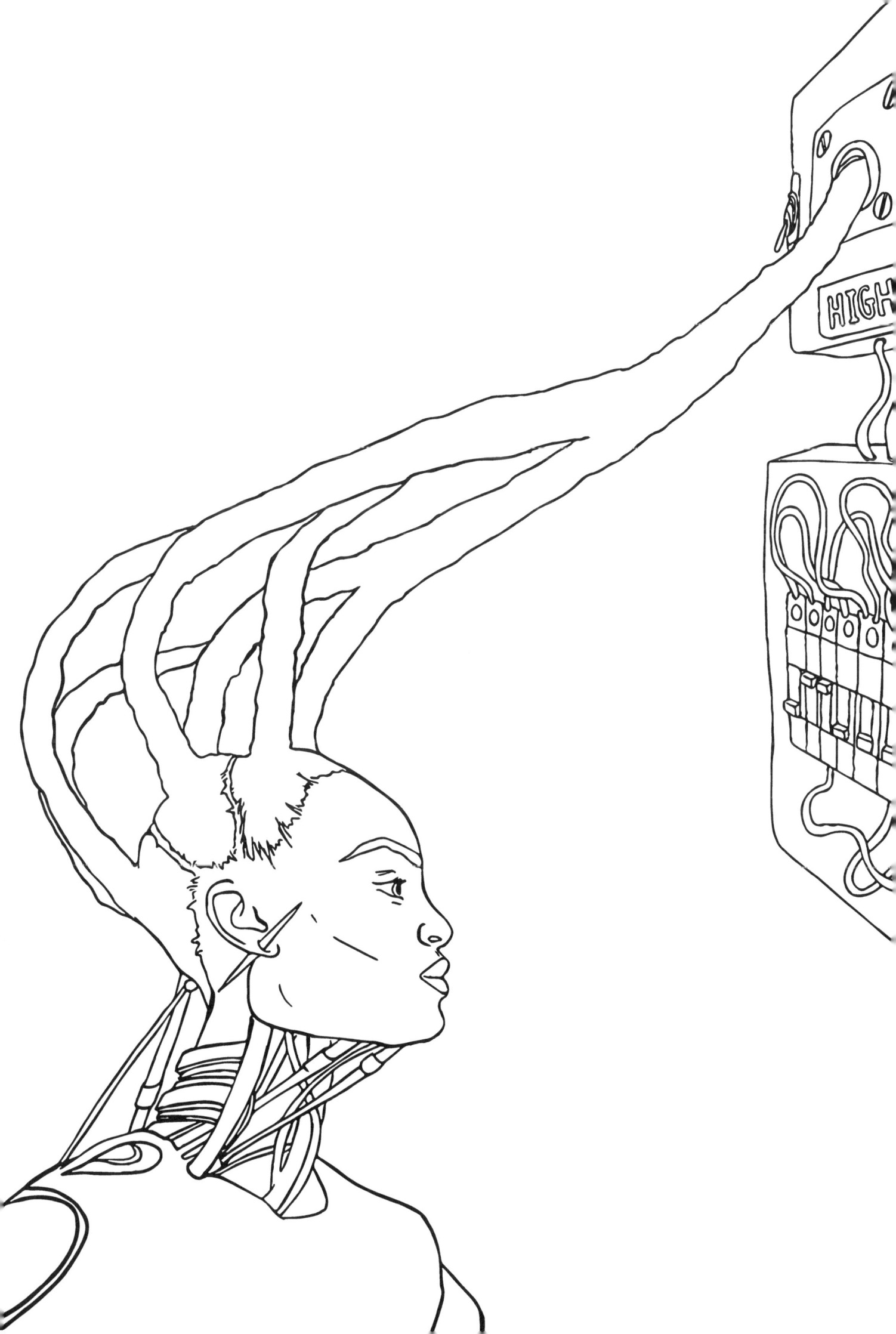

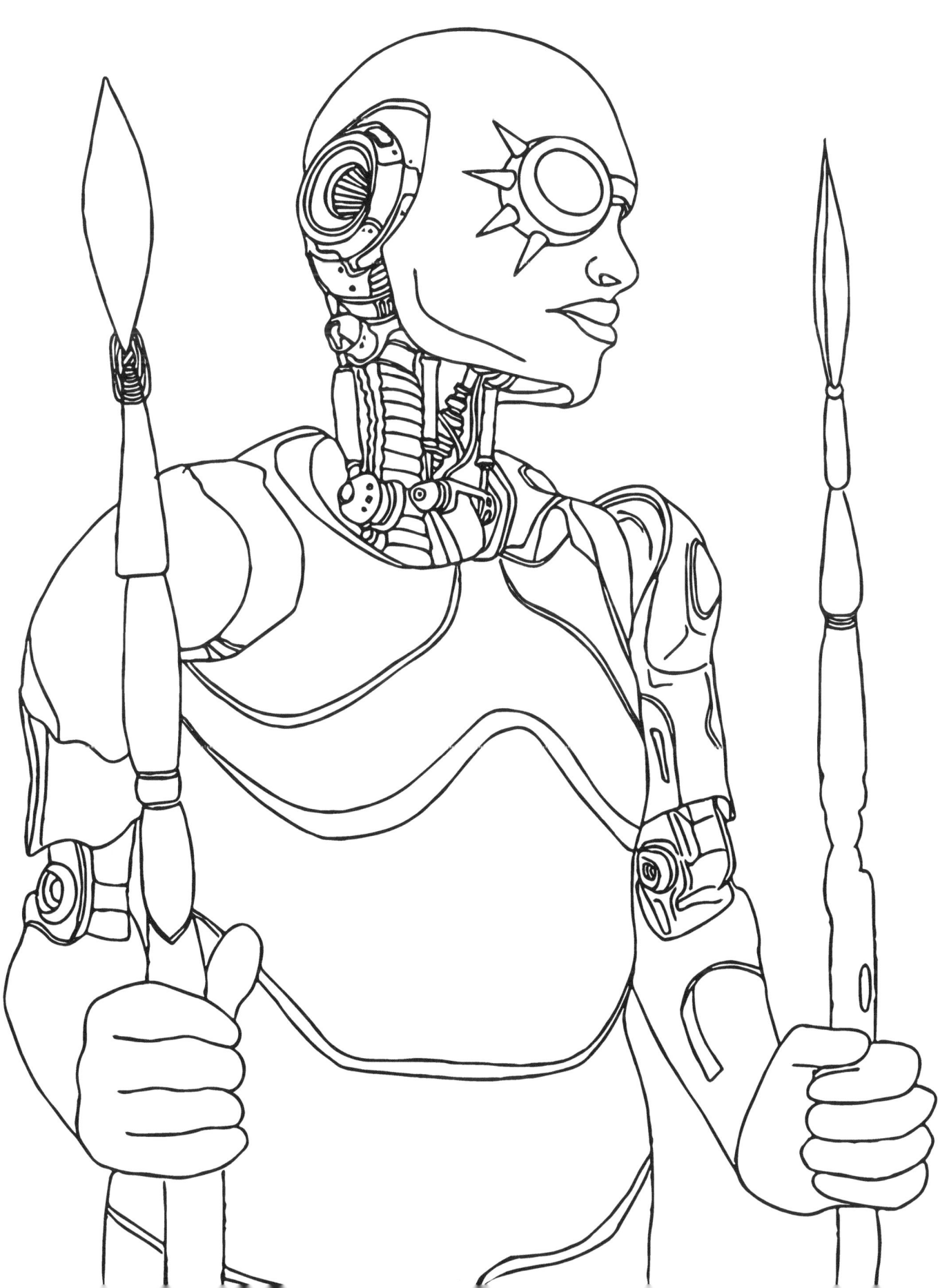

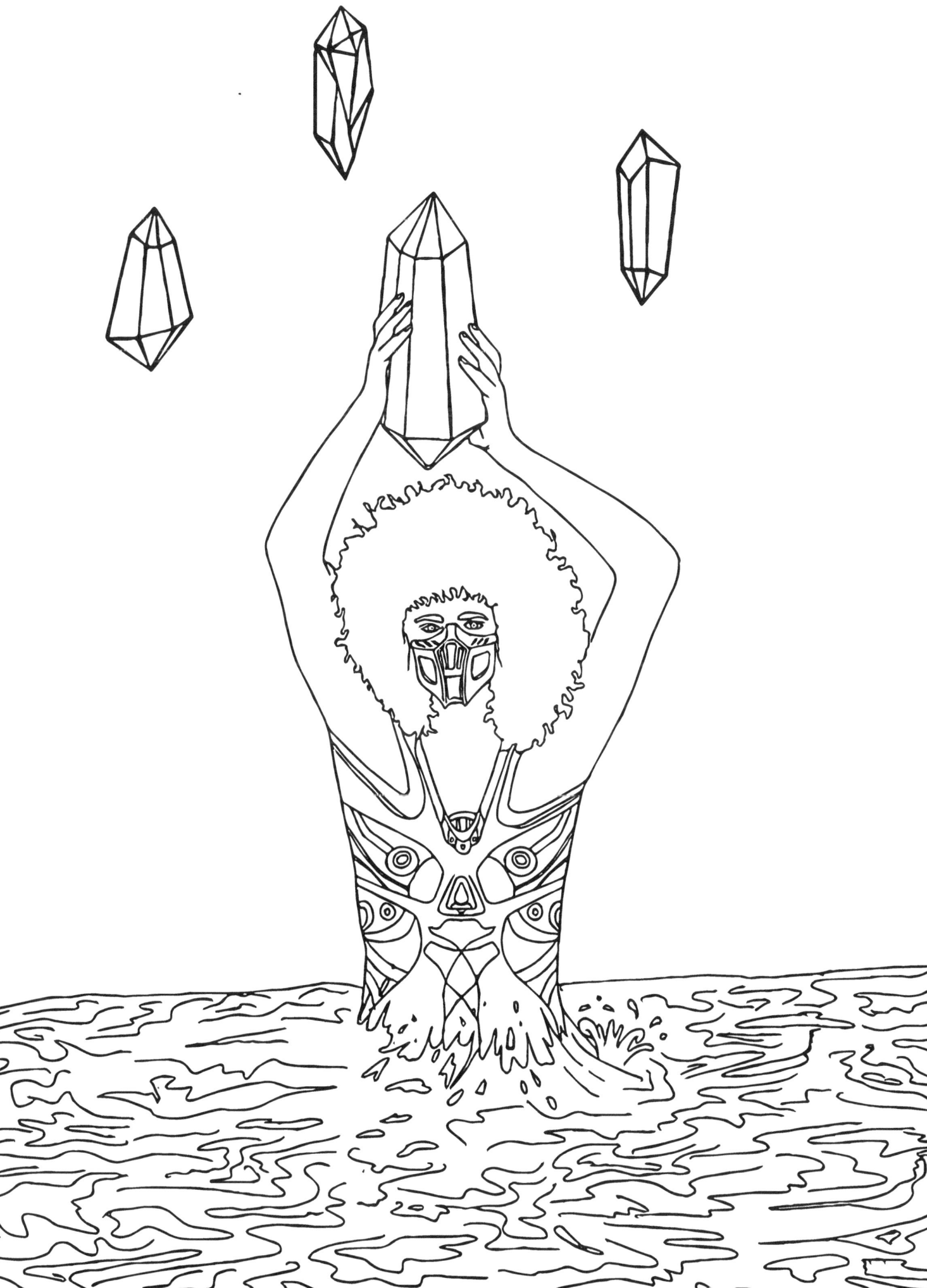

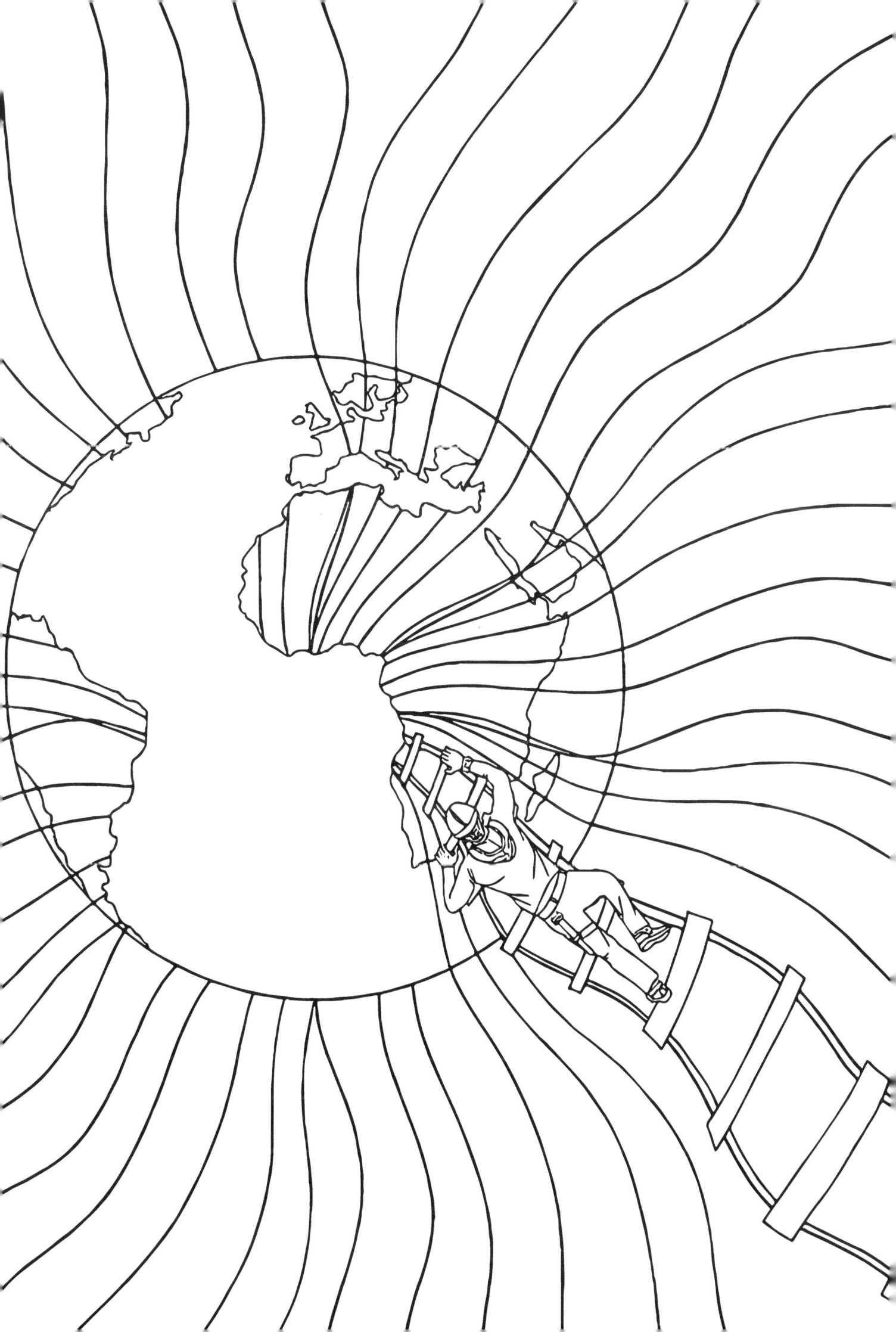